The WILDERNESS of SUICIDE GRIEF

Also by Alan Wolfelt:

Healing Your Grieving Heart: 100 Practical Ideas

Healing A Friend's Grieving Heart: 100 Practical Ideas for Helping Someone You Love Through Loss

The Journey Through Grief: Reflections on Healing

Understanding Your Suicide Grief: Ten Essential Touchstones for Finding Hope and Healing Your Heart

The Understanding Your Suicide Grief Journal: Exploring the Ten Essential Touchstones

Companion
P R E S S

Companion Press is dedicated to the education and support of both the bereaved and bereavement caregivers. We believe that those who companion the bereaved by walking with them as they journey in grief have a wondrous opportunity: to help others embrace and grow through grief—and to lead fuller, more deeply-lived lives themselves because of this important ministry.

For a complete catalog and ordering information, write or call:

Companion Press
The Center for Loss and Life Transition
3735 Broken Bow Road Fort Collins, CO 80526
(970) 226-6050
www.centerforloss.com

The WILDERNESS of SUICIDE GRIEF
Finding Your Way

Alan D. Wolfelt, Ph.D.

Companion
PRESS
Fort Collins, Colorado
An imprint of the Center for Loss and Life Transition

Companion Press is an imprint of the
Center for Loss and Life Transition,
3735 Broken Bow Road, Fort Collins, Colorado 80526
970-226-6050
www.centerforloss.com

Cover design and book layout by Angela P. Hollingsworth

Printed in the United States of America.

22   5 4

ISBN: 978-1-879651-68-5

Contents

Introduction 9

Touchstone One
Open to the Presence of Your Loss 13

Touchstone Two
Dispel the Misconceptions About Suicide and
Grief and Mourning 23

Touchstone Three
Embrace the Uniqueness of Your Suicide Grief 35

Touchstone Four
Explore Your Feelings of Loss 45

Touchstone Five
Recognize You Are Not Crazy 63

Touchstone Six
Understand the Six Needs of Mourning 79

Touchstone Seven
Nurture Yourself 89

Touchstone Eight
Reach Out for Help 101

Touchstone Nine
Seek Reconciliation, Not Resolution 109

Touchstone Ten
Appreciate Your Transformation 117

The Suicide Survivor's Bill of Rights 125

"Take this sorrow to thy heart, and make it a part of thee, and it shall nourish thee till though art strong again."

- Longfellow

Welcome:
An Invitation to Open Your Heart

You are heartbroken, and your entire being literally aches physically, emotionally, and spiritually from the pain of the loss of someone who was precious to you. As you slowly read and reflect on the content of this book, I hope and pray that you find some sense of comfort and support.

The suicide death of a friend or family member is never our choice, yet we are faced with the need to confront our raw and life-changing grief. Yet for a number of reasons, we may not know how or where or if we should express the pain that comes with this profound loss. As you will learn throughout this book, the only way to eventually heal is to mourn.

Think of your grief as a wilderness—a vast, mountainous, inhospitable forest. You are in the wilderness now. You are in the midst of unfamiliar and often brutal surroundings. You are cold and tired. You must journey through this wilderness.

Yet, as you do so, remember: go slowly. There are no rewards for speed! As you slowly find your way out of this wilderness experience, you must become acquainted with its terrain and learn to follow the sometimes hard-to-find trail that leads to healing.

In the wilderness of your grief, the ten Touchstones are your trail markers. They are the signs that let you know you are on the right path. I also like to think of them as "wisdom teachings" that the many people I have supported following a suicide death have taught me.

Those who have gone before you and me have indeed left us many trail markers that show us how they made it through the wilderness of suicide grief. If we look, we will see that they have been gracious enough to pass them on to others who enter this inhospitable wilderness. Others have gone before us and discovered the strength not only to survive, but eventually to thrive. From the depths of my being, I believe you can too.

And even when you've become a master journeyer and you know well the terrain of your grief, you will at times feel like you are backtracking and being ravaged by the forces around you. This, too, is the nature of grief after a death to suicide. Complete mastery of a wilderness is not possible. Just as we cannot control the winds and the storms and the beasts in nature, we can never have total dominion over our grief.

But if you do the work of mourning, if you become an intrepid traveler on your journey, if you make use of these ten Touchstones, I promise you that you will find your way out of the wilderness of your grief and you will learn to have renewed meaning and purpose in your precious life.

Open to the Presence of Your Loss

"In every heart there is an inner room, where we can hold our greatest treasures and our deepest pain."

- Marianne Williamson

Someone you love has completed suicide. In your heart, you have come to know your deepest pain. To be "bereaved" literally means "to be torn apart." You have a broken heart, and your life has been turned upside down.

While it is instinctive to want to run as far away as possible from the overwhelming pain that comes with this loss, you have probably already discovered that even if you try to hide, deny, or self-treat your pain, it is still within you, demanding your attention. In acknowledging the inevitability of the pain and raw suffering that come with this grief, in coming to understand the need to gently embrace the pain, you in effect honor the pain.

The word *honor* literally means recognizing the value of and respecting. It is not instinctive to see the grief that erupts following a suicide death and the need to mourn as things to honor. But I hope you discover, as I have, that to honor your grief is not self-destructive or harmful, it is self-sustaining and life-giving.

You have probably been taught that pain is an indication that something is wrong and that you should find a way to alleviate the pain. In our culture, the role of pain and suffering is misunderstood. This is particularly true with suicide grief. Because of the stigma and taboo surrounding suicide, many people think you shouldn't talk about it, let alone honor your pain by openly mourning.

In part, this book will encourage you to be present to your multitude of thoughts and feelings, to "be with" them, for they contain the truth you are searching for, the energy you may be lacking, and the unfolding of your eventual healing.

Setting Your Intention to Heal

It takes a true commitment to heal in your grief. Yes, you are wounded, but with commitment and intention you can and will become whole again. Intention is defined as being conscious of what you want to experience. A close cousin to "affirmation," it is using the power of positive thought to produce a desired result.

When you set your intention to heal, you make a true commitment to positively influence the course of your journey. You probably know the cliché: "Time heals all wounds." Yet, time alone does not heal the wounds of grief that come with suicide. I like to remind myself and other survivors that healing waits on welcome, not on time! Healing and integrating this loss into your life demand that you engage actively in the grief journey.

A Vital Distinction: Shock Versus Denial

Shock, along with elements of denial, is a temporary, healthy response that essentially says, "The reality of the suicide death of someone dear to me is too painful to acknowledge right now. Therefore I refuse to believe it." *While this is a natural initial reaction to suicide, you will hinder your eventual healing if you stay in long-term denial.*

There are various forms of denial that, as a survivor, you must work to break through:

Conscious Denial: This is where you hide the fact that the death was suicide. You may tell people it was a heart attack, murder, or an unexplained sudden death.

<u>Innocent Denial</u>: This is where you hold onto the hope that the findings that ruled the death a suicide were a mistake and will be changed at a later date.

<u>Blame as Denial</u>: This is where you blame someone else for the suicide, thereby denying the choice someone made to take his or her own life.

<u>Pretense and Denial</u>: This is where the unwritten family rule is that you never talk about the death or use the word *suicide* at any time.

The motivations for these types of denial are multiple and complex. Often, people don't even realize they are in denial. So, if you discover you have gone beyond shock into some form of prolonged denial, do not shame or ridicule yourself.

But here is the problem: By staying in denial, you miss the opportunity to do the grief work related to your feelings. Until denial is broken through and the pain is experienced, you are on hold and authentic mourning cannot take place.

Face Any Inappropriate Expectations

You are at risk for having inappropriate expectations about this death. These expectations result from common societal messages that tell you to "be strong" in the face of life losses. Invariably, some well-intentioned people around you will urge you to "move on," "let go," "keep your chin up," and "keep busy." Actually, you need to give yourself as much time as you need to mourn, and these kinds of comments hurt you, not help you.

Society often makes mourners feel shame or embarrassment about our feelings of grief, particularly suicide grief. It implies that if you, as a grieving person, openly express your feeling of grief, you are being immature. If your feelings are fairly intense, you may be labeled overly emotional or needy. If your feelings are extremely intense, you may even be referred to as crazy or a "pathological mourner."

As a professional grief counselor, I assure you that you are not immature, overly emotional, or crazy. But the societal messages surrounding grief that you may receive are!

If you fear emotions and see them as negative, you will be at risk for crying alone and in private. Yet, being secretive with your emotions doesn't integrate your painful feelings of loss; it complicates them. Then even more pain comes from trying to keep the pain secret. You cannot hide your feelings *and* find renewed meaning in your life. If you are dishonest about your pain, you stay in pain.

Grief Is Not a Disease

You have probably already discovered that no quick fix exists for the pain you are enduring. Grief following a suicide is naturally complex, and it is easy to feel overwhelmed. But I promise you that if you can think, feel, and see yourself as an active participant in your healing, you will slowly but surely experience a renewed sense of meaning and purpose in your life.

Grief is not a disease. To be human means coming to know loss as part of your life. While the grief that accompanies suicide is a powerful, life-changing experience, so, too, is your ability to help facilitate your own healing.

I invite you to gently confront the pain of your grief. Be open to the miracle of healing. Integrating the grief that comes with a suicide death requires your willingness. You must have willingness or you would not have picked up this book. Follow your willingness and allow it to bless you.

In large part, healing from a suicide death is anchored in a decision to not judge yourself but to love yourself. Grief is a call for love. So, if you are judging yourself and where you are in this journey, STOP! When you stop judging the multitude of emotions that come with your grief, you are left with acceptance, and when you have acceptance (or surrender), you have love. Love will lead you into and through the wilderness, to a place where you will come out of the dark and into the light.

Dispel the Misconceptions About Suicide and Grief and Mourning

Misconception: A misconception is a mistaken notion you might have about something—in other words, something you believe to be true but that is not true. Misconceptions about grief are common in our society because we tend not to openly mourn or talk about grief and mourning. You can see how we'd have misconceptions about something as "in the closet" as suicide grief.

As you journey through the wilderness of your suicide grief, if you mourn openly and authentically, you will come to find a path that feels right for you. But beware—others may try to pull you off this path. They may try to make you believe that the path you have chosen is wrong—even crazy—and that their way is better.

They have internalized some common misconceptions about suicide grief and mourning. And the misconceptions, in essence, deny you your right to hurt and authentically express your grief.

As you read about this important Touchstone, you may discover that you yourself have believed in some of the misconceptions and that some may be embraced by people around you. Don't condemn yourself or others for having believed in them. Simply make use of any new insights to help you open your heart to your work of mourning in ways that restore your soul.

Misconception: Grief and mourning are the same thing.

Perhaps you have noticed that people tend to use the words "grieving" and "mourning" interchangeably. There is an important distinction, however. *Grief* is the constellation of internal thoughts and feelings you have when someone you love dies. *Mourning* is when you take the grief you have on the inside and express it outside of yourself. Over time and with the support of others, to mourn is to heal.

WARNING: After someone you love has completed suicide, your friends may encourage you to keep your grief to yourself. A catalyst for healing, however, can only be created when you develop the courage to mourn publicly, in the presence of understanding, compassionate people who will not judge you.

Misconception: Grief following a suicide death always results in "complicated" or "pathological" mourning.

Research indicates that survivors of suicide integrate grief at about the same pace as those who experience any kind of unanticipated death. Obviously, there can be some natural challenges, such as the combination of sudden shock, the natural question of "why?", the trauma of witnessing or discovering the suicide, the lack of support from family and friends, and the potential of "secondary victimization" that results from cruel, judgmental, or insensitive comments from others, but do not let this misconception become a self-fulfilling prophecy. Do your work of mourning, and you will come out of the dark and into the light.

Misconception: Grief and mourning
progress in predictable, orderly stages.

The concept of stages was popularized in 1969 with the publication of Elisabeth Kübler-Ross's landmark text *On Death and Dying*. However, Dr. Kübler-Ross never intended for her stages to be interpreted as a rigid, linear sequence to be followed by all mourners.

As a grieving person, you will probably encounter others who have adopted a rigid system of beliefs about what you should experience in your grief journey. And if you have internalized this misconception, you may also find yourself trying to prescribe your own grief experience as well.

Everyone mourns in different ways. Personal experience is your best teacher about where you are in your grief journey. Don't think your goal is to move through prescribed stages of grief.

Misconception: We can always determine
the "whys?" of a suicide death.

Why the person took his or her own life can be a painful yet natural question to explore, yet it's a question for which there is often no clear, satisfactory answer. My experience with many survivors suggests that you may very slowly, with no rewards for speed, discover that it is possible to live with the uncertainty of never fully knowing the answer to "why?"

Misconception: All suicide survivors feel guilty.

The sad reality is that some people will actually say directly to you, "I bet you feel guilty" or pose the question, "Do you feel guilty?" This is one of the most prescribed responses for survivors of suicide. In reality, as a survivor you may or may not feel guilty. Besides, assuming you feel guilt is the opposite of my belief that you are the expert of your own experience and therefore you must teach me what you feel; I must not prescribe what you *should* feel.

Misconception: Only certain kinds of people complete suicide.

This is a simple misconception to dispel. The reality is that suicide is a stranger to no race, creed, religion, age group, or socioeconomic level. All kinds of people have completed suicide since the beginning of recorded history.

Misconception: Only a crazy person completes suicide.

While the person you loved who completed suicide may have been depressed, anxious, or hopeless, to be sure, most of us survivors don't find comfort when people try to tell us the person was crazy. Not all people who complete suicide meet some formal criteria for mental illness, and even when they do, we don't need to hear that they were crazy.

Misconception: It is a sin to complete suicide, and the person who does goes directly to hell.

As one Catholic priest observed about suicide, "When its victims wake on the other side, they are met by a gentle Christ who stands right inside of their huddled fear and says, 'Peace be with you!' As we see in the gospels, God can go through locked doors, breathe out peace in places where we cannot get in, and write straight with even the most crooked of lines."

Personally, I believe there are no limits to God's compassion. God mourns with us. If God's nature is one of steadfast mercy and love, then this is a misconception we need to keep educating the world about.

Misconception: Suicide is inherited and runs in the family.

Be alert for uninformed people who may project to you that because someone in your family completed suicide, you may have the same fate. This projection is not supported by the facts. Scientific research has not at this time confirmed a genetic basis for suicide risk.

Misconception: Tears of grief are
only a sign of weakness.

Tears of grief are often associated with personal inadequacy
and weakness. The worst thing you can do, however, is to
allow this judgment to prevent you from crying.

Sometimes, the people who care about you may, directly
or indirectly, try to prevent your tears out of a desire to
protect you (and them) from pain. You may hear comments
like, "Tears won't bring him back" or "He wouldn't want
you to cry." Yet crying is nature's way of releasing internal
tension in your body, and it allows you to communicate a
need to be comforted.

Misconception: Being upset and openly mourning
means you are being weak in your faith.

Watch out for those who think that having faith and
openly mourning are mutually exclusive. If you are mad
at God, be mad at God. Similarly, if you need a time-out
from regular worship, don't shame yourself. When and
if you are ready, attending a church, synagogue, or other
place of worship, reading scripture, and praying are only

a few ways you might want to express your faith. Or, you may be open to less conventional ways, such as meditating or spending time alone in nature.

Misconception: When someone you love completes suicide, you only grieve and mourn for the physical loss of the person.

When someone you love completes suicide, you don't just lose the presence of that person. As a result of the death, you may lose many other connections to yourself and the world around you. These secondary losses can include:

Loss of self
- self ("I feel like part of me died when he died.")
- identity (You may have to rethink your role as husband or wife, mother or father, son or daughter, best friend, etc.)
- self-confidence (Some grievers experience lowered self-esteem. Naturally, you may have lost one of the people in your life who gave you confidence.)
- health (Physical symptoms of mourning.)
- personality ("I just don't feel like myself...")
- fiscal security (You may have financial concerns or

have to learn to manage finances in ways you didn't
before.)
- lifestyle (Your lifestyle has changed and no longer feels
safe.)

Loss of meaning
- goals and dreams (Hopes and dreams for the future
can be shattered.)
- faith (You may question your faith.)
- will/desire to live (You may have questions related to
future meaning in your life. You may ask, "Why go
on...?")
- joy (Life's most precious emotion, happiness, is
naturally compromised by the death of someone we
love.)

Allowing yourself to acknowledge the many levels of loss
the suicide death has brought to your life will help you
continue to stay open to your unique grief journey.

Now that we've reviewed the common misconceptions of
grief, let's wrap up Touchstone Two by listing some of the
"conceptions." These are some realities you can hold onto
as you journey toward healing.

Realistic expectations for grief and mourning

- You will naturally grieve, but you will probably have to make a conscious effort to mourn.
- Your grief and mourning will involve a wide variety of different thoughts and feelings.
- Your grief and mourning will impact you in all five realms of experience: physical; emotional; cognitive; social; and spiritual.
- You need to feel it to heal it.
- Your grief will probably hurt more before it hurts less.
- Your grief will be unpredictable and will not likely progress in an orderly fashion.
- You don't "get over" grief; you learn to live with it.
- You need other people to help you through your grief.
- You will not always feel this bad.

Embrace the Uniqueness
of Your Suicide Grief

"The most authentic thing about us is our capacity to create, to overcome, to endure, to transform, to love, and to be greater than our suffering."

- Ben Okri

When suicide impacts our lives, we all need to grieve, and, as you learned in Touchstone Two, to mourn. But our grief journeys are never exactly the same. Despite what you may hear, you will do the work of mourning in your own unique way. This Touchstone invites you to explore some of the unique reasons your grief is what it is—the "whys" of your journey through the wilderness.

Why #1: The circumstances of the suicide

A suicide death is often very traumatic. The combination of sudden shock and the stigma of suicide result in a kind of psychic numbing to your spirit.

The particular circumstances of suicide may also contribute to the uniqueness of your grief. For example, suicide deaths often initially have to be investigated as if a crime may have taken place. Life insurance problems, media coverage unpleasantness, and other issues may arise. Some people around you may put more focus on the act of suicide itself than on the importance of supporting you. Sometimes the first question people ask is, "How did he do it?"

The list of potential circumstances surrounding suicide grief are multiple and complex. I imagine there are some additional influences you can think of. Whatever your unique challenges, you will be well served to explore them and see how they shape the terrain of your journey.

Why #2: Your relationship with the person who completed suicide

Obviously, the relationship you had with the person who completed suicide will have a major influence on your grief experience. Maybe you were very close, or perhaps you had a very difficult relationship with this person. Whatever the circumstances, you are the best person to describe and work toward understanding your relationship with the person who died.

Why #3: The people in your life

Mourning the death of someone to suicide requires the outside support of other human beings. Because suicide is a topic where many people don't know how to support you, some people in your world will probably pull away. This potential lack of support can be painful and agonizing.

The good news is that even one compassionate, supportive person can be a real difference-maker. Find a trusted family member, friend, fellow survivor, or sensitive counselor to companion you through the terrain of your grief. This person can and will help you survive at a time when you are not sure you can.

Why #4: Your unique personality

Whatever your unique personality, rest assured it will be reflected in your grief. For example, if you are quiet by nature, you may express your grief quietly. If you tend to be expressive, you may openly express how you feel about your grief.

Keep in mind there is no one right and only way to mourn. Part of your experience will be to accept that you are mourning in ways that reflect your unique personality.

Why #5: The unique personality of the person who completed suicide

Just as your own personality is reflected in your grief journey, so, too, is the unique personality of the person who completed suicide. Whatever your feelings are about the personality of the person who completed suicide, find someone who will encourage you to talk about him or her openly and honestly. Authentic mourning requires you be open about what you miss and what you don't miss. If you don't have someone who can listen to you, write about it in a journal.

Why #6: Your gender

Your gender may not only influence your grief, but also the way others relate to you. Men are often more stoic, while women tend to be more open with their feelings. Still, we must be careful when it comes to generalizations about gender differences. Sometimes too much is made of the difference between genders and not enough is made of the organic capacity to grieve and mourn. Once you welcome mourning into your heart, your willingness and capacity to mourn often transcend gender.

Why #7: Your cultural/ethnic/religious/spiritual background

Your cultural and ethnic background as well as your personal belief system can have a tremendous impact on your journey into grief. When I say culture, I mean the values, rules (spoken and unspoken), and traditions that guide you and your family.

As you are probably aware, suicide has a long and complex history with religion. It wasn't all that long ago that suicide was thought to be a sin by almost all major faiths. Thank God that in contemporary times, many (but not all) communities of faith offer compassion and support to survivors.

Let me be very direct with you—if you turn to a clergyperson for support and he or she tells you that suicide is an unpardonable sin, go someplace else to get the support and non-judgment you both need and deserve.

Why #8: Other changes, crises, or stresses in your life right now

Whatever your specific situation, I imagine your grief is not the only stress in your life right now. You may well feel like your life is in total chaos. That is why you will want to pay special attention to the importance of nurturing yourself and reaching out for and accepting help. Allow me to gently remind you to be patient and self-nurturing during this time of overwhelming grief in your life.

Why #9: The funeral or ritual experience after the death

The funeral is a time and a place to express your feelings about the death, thus legitimizing them. The funeral also can serve as a time to honor the person who has died, bring you closer to others who can give you needed support, affirm that life goes on even in the face of death, and give you a context of meaning that is in keeping with your own religious, spiritual, or philosophical background.

Following a sudden, traumatic death, however, the funeral experience often feels—in hindsight—unsatisfactory. It may feel to you now that it was haphazardly planned or incomplete. Your natural shock at the time may have prevented you from feeling as if you were even really "there." Rest assured that it is never too late after a death for you to plan and implement a ritual (even a second or third ceremony) that will help meet your needs. I call these "corrective emotional-spiritual experiences." You might choose to have a tree planting ceremony in the spring, for example, in honor of the person who died. Or you might elect to hold a memorial service on the anniversary of the death. You deserve to have a meaningful ceremony, and so does the person who died.

Why #10: Your physical health

How you feel physically has a significant effect on your grief. We know that your immune system is compromised when you experience death loss, particularly a sudden, traumatic death. Perhaps you have an existing illness that was already impacting your life. If you are physically ill, your bodily symptoms may actually inhibit some of your capacity to mourn at emotional and spiritual levels.

From Mourning the "Whys" Of your
Journey to the "Whats"

The "whys" of your journey have, I hope and trust, been
helpful for you to explore in Touchstone Three. Now we
can go on the explore what feelings or responses you are
having based on these influences.

TOUCHSTONE FOUR

Explore Your
Feelings of Loss

"Stepping into the wilderness of your many feelings of grief is an important and sacred part of your life right now. It is my experience that we cannot heal what we cannot feel or do not allow ourselves to feel."

- Alan D. Wolfelt

Suicide is synonymous with disruption, chaos, and change—all of which bring a multitude of overwhelming emotions. Taking ownership of your wilderness emotions is the only way to eventually re-orient and survive this life-changing experience. Be patient, steadfast, and self-compassionate as we explore this important Touchstone.

The Importance of Experiencing and Expressing Your Feelings

As overwhelming as your emotions may seem, they are true expressions of where you are in the terrain of your journey. Rather than deny, inhibit, self-treat, or go around them (all of which can be tempting), I want to help you recognize and learn from them.

Some people ask me, "What is the point of experiencing and expressing feelings if they don't change anything?"

It's true that experiencing and talking about your feelings does not change what you are going through. However, self-expression does have the capacity to change you and the way you see the world around you.

Authentic mourning creates what is called *perturbation*, which is "the capacity to experience change and movement." The word *feeling* originates from the Indo-European root that literally means "touch." So, it is in expressing your feelings that you activate your capacity to be touched and changed by experiences you encounter along life's path. If you deny, inhibit, or self-treat your feelings, your pain will actually last longer.

Please don't think of your feelings as "negative;" instead, think of them as necessary. If you perceive some of your feelings, such as anger, sadness, and anxiety, as negative, you will not gain anything helpful from them.

My hope is that this Touchstone will help you see how *natural* your many thoughts, feelings, and behaviors are. The eventual healing that we experience as survivors is not a task, it is a need. It simply requires our willingness. Follow your willingness and allow it to bless you, and allow your willingness to bring the miracle of healing to you!

Shock, Numbness, Denial, and Disbelief

"It feels like a dream," people in early grief from a suicide death often say. "I feel like I might wake up and this will not have happened."

Thank goodness for shock, numbness, and disbelief! Other words that survivors use to describe their initial grief are *dazed* and *stunned*. These feelings are nature's way of temporarily protecting you from the full reality of the sudden, tragic death. They help insulate you psychologically until you are more able to tolerate what you don't want to believe.

Trauma loss from suicide often goes beyond what might be considered "normal" shock. In fact, you may experience what is called "psychic numbing"—the deadening or shutting off of emotions. Your sense that "this isn't happening to me" often continues much longer than with other circumstances of death.

Especially in the beginning of your grief journey, your emotions need time to catch up with what your mind has been told. Even when it is clear that the death was from suicide, you may find yourself needing to deny this fact. In a very real sense, it is a way of holding off the pain and suffering that is coming soon enough.

Be compassionate with yourself. Allow for this instinctive form of self-protection. And reach out for support from caring friends, family, fellow survivors, and sensitive caregivers you trust.

Disorganization, Confusion, Searching, and Yearning

Perhaps the most isolating and frightening part of your grief journey is the sense of disorganization, confusion, searching, and yearning that often comes with the death of someone you love to suicide.

You may feel a sense of restlessness, agitation, impatience, and ongoing confusion. It's like being in the middle of a wild, rushing river where you can't get a grasp on anything. Disconnected thoughts may race through your mind, and a multitude of strong emotions may be overwhelming. This is usually accompanied by what is called *anhedonia*—the inability to find joy in things that previously brought you joy.

If you discovered the body or witnessed the death, this part of your grief can be naturally complicated. If your mind is impacted by recurring and unwanted images, please seek help immediately from someone trained to assist you.

During this time you may experience a shift in perception; other people may begin to look like the person in your life who completed suicide. You might be at a shopping mall, look down a hallway, and think you see the person. Or you might see a familiar car drive past and find yourself wanting to drive after the car.

As part of your searching and yearning, you may not only experience a sense of the dead person's presence, but you also may have fleeting glimpses of the person across a room.

The thoughts, feelings, and behaviors of this dimension do not come all at once. They are often experienced in a wave-like fashion. You might have a day or even several days where you feel more focused again, and then your disorganization and confusion return suddenly and without notice. This is natural, so I urge you to not get discouraged.

When you feel disoriented, talk to someone who will be supportive and understanding. Sometimes when you talk, you may not think you make much sense. But talking it out can still be self-clarifying, even at a subconscious level.

Anxiety, Fear, and Panic

Feelings of anxiety, fear, and panic may be part of your grief experience. You may ask yourself, "Will I survive this? Will I be so overwhelmed that I, too, would take my own life? What about other family members? Might they take their own lives? Will my life have any meaning and purpose without this person?" These questions are natural. Your sense of safety and security has been threatened, and you are naturally anxious.

You now know the pain and devastation that suicide brings into the lives of survivors. The fact that you are taking time to read this book demonstrates your desire to integrate this loss into your life and go on living. If any thoughts persist around fear of taking your own life, I plead with you to go see a professional caregiver who can assist you right now!

While unpleasant, anxiety, fear, and yes, even panic, can be natural components of the grief experience. The good news is that expressing your fears can help make them more tolerable. Also, recognizing that they are temporary and will soften over time can and will help you during this vulnerable time in your life.

Consider deep breathing exercises to help you with anxiety. Journaling, if it is a good match for you, can be a powerful way to help track your progress. It also allows you to get thoughts on paper instead of holding them in your head, where they are more likely to keep getting in the way. Finally, remember that building in a regular exercise program can do wonders to help with anxiety.

Explosive Emotions

Anger, blame, terror, even rage are explosive emotions that may be part of your experience. Some survivors have taught me they find them frightening, particularly when they are focused on the person who has completed suicide.

Your explosive feelings are, fundamentally, a form of protest. It is psycho-biologically instinctive in the face of traumatic loss to protest—to dislike your new reality and want to change it in some way.

You may direct your instinctive need to protest toward the person who completed suicide. "How could you abandon me, your family, your friends, and give up on living!" You may be mad at God. You may be mad at friends, family members, investigative officers, or anyone who is available.

It makes good sense that the emotional defense against fear is anger. This entire experience doesn't feel *fair* or *right*. It feels *unfair* and *all wrong*! Anger and other explosive emotions can help you feel you have some element of control at a time when you naturally feel out of control. They also help counter more passive, painful feelings of despair and sadness.

Some people around you may try to convince you that demonstrating any kind of emotional or spiritual protest is wrong. They may say you should just "accept" what has happened and "get on with your life." Yet, as you have come to realize, it is not that easy. When you do show symptoms of protest, there are bound to be some people around you who may perceive you as being "out of control" or "not handling your grief" very well.

Yet you must give yourself permission to feel whatever you feel and to express those feelings. If explosive emotions are part of your journey (and they aren't for everyone), be aware that you have two avenues for expression—outward or inward. The outward avenue leads to eventual healing and transformation; the inward does not. Keeping your explosive emotions inside often leads to low self-esteem, depression, anxiety disorders, guilt, physical complaints, and sometimes even persistent thoughts of self-destruction.

Guilt, Regret, Self-Blame, Shame, and Embarrassment

This constellation of potential feelings *may* be a part of the emotional rollercoaster of your grief experience. Some of these feelings may apply to you, while others may not. Also, a very important warning: Some people will project that you SHOULD feel guilty. I've always found it interesting that we don't automatically *prescribe* guilt in other circumstances of death (cancer, accidents, etc.), yet I often hear people say to survivors of suicide, "I bet you feel guilty." Well, some survivors do and some survivors don't, so we should not make this assumption.

Allow me to be very direct: You are not responsible for anyone's decision to complete suicide. The simple reality is that only one person is responsible for the completion of suicide: the person who did so.

Still, when someone you care about takes his or her own life, it's natural to think about actions you could or could not have taken to prevent the death. It's natural to explore your "If onlys" and "What ifs."

I cannot emphasize enough that it will be vitally important to work through any and all aspects of guilt, regret, shame,and self-blame you might feel. Why? Because guilt can become a way of life built upon belief of your own personal *unworthiness*. Then you risk becoming among the living dead. Because as long as you judge yourself as unworthy, you will never be able to fully integrate this grief into your life and discover renewed meaning and purpose.

If you shroud the reality of this suicide death in secrecy, realize that where there is shame, there will be chronic pain. In effect, you will experience as much unhappiness and chronic sadness as you believe you deserve.

By being honest about the suicide and embracing the reality that only one person is responsible for the suicide (the person who did it), the pain you feel can begin to soften. Opening yourself to any internalized shame, the pain and sadness you carry begin to melt and you discover you are no longer alone and help is just waiting for you.

Sadness, Depression, Loneliness, and Vulnerability

Some of the most natural aspects of grief following suicide are sadness, depression, loneliness, and vulnerability. Someone precious in your life is now gone. Of course you are sad. Of course you feel deep sorrow. Allowing yourself to feel your sadness is in large part what your journey toward healing is all about.

These emotions are often experienced in a series of roller-coaster cycles, sometimes up, sometimes down. One day may seem survivable and hopeful; the next day you may be caught in an overwhelming wave of deep sadness. As life goes forward, you may feel incredibly vulnerable.

Weeks, or often months, will pass before you are fully confronted by the depths of your sorrow. The slow-growing nature of this is good. You could not and should not try to tolerate all of your sadness at once. Your body, mind, and spirit need time to work together to embrace the depth of your loss. Please be patient with yourself.

This is a time of many changes and instability. You are in what is called "liminal space." *Limina* is the Latin word for threshold, the space betwixt and between. Liminal space is that spiritual place you hate to be, but where the experience of suicide grief often takes you.

Sometimes your feelings of sadness and sorrow can be overwhelming enough to be classified as clinical depression. After all, the mourning that comes with a death to suicide can share many symptoms with depression, including sleep disturbances, appetite changes, decreased energy, withdrawal, guilt, dependency, lack of concentration, and a sense of loss of control. You may have a hard time functioning at home and at work, which may compound your feelings of isolation, helplessness, and vulnerability. If you are feeling totally immobilized by depression, please get some help from a professional grief counselor sensitive to the trauma of suicide grief immediately.

Paradoxically, the only way to eventually lessen your pain is to move toward it, not away from it. To be able to move toward these feelings requires that you find and make use of compassionate people to whom you can express your authentic feelings. Talk openly with compassionate friends and family about where you see yourself surrounding these feelings outlined above. You need people to affirm and support you right now. You need people who will sometimes walk with you—not behind or in front of you, but beside you—on your path through the wilderness.

If talking is an avenue that works for you, keep talking until you have exhausted your capacity to talk. Doing so will help reconnect you to the world outside of yourself. Or, if you can't talk it out, write it out! Paint it out! Sing it out! But get the feelings outside of yourself. And, if fitting with your personality, give yourself permission to cry—as often and as much as you need to. Tears can help cleanse you body, mind, and spirit.

Relief and Release

Some suicide survivors have taught me they sometimes feel a sense of relief and release after the death. Perhaps the person had suffered a long, debilitating decline over many years. Another form of relief sometimes occurs when the person who completed suicide had an extensive history of having threatened or attempted suicide many times before the actual act.

When appropriate, allowing yourself to acknowledge relief as part of your grief experience can be a critical step in your journey through grief. Whatever your feelings, working to embrace them creates the opportunity to find hope in your healing. Remember—relief does not equal a lack of concern or love for the person who is now dead. Whatever you do, don't deny feelings of relief if you have them. They deserve to be honored just like any of the other feelings you have!

A Final Thought About The Feelings You May Experience

As you journey through the wilderness of your suicide grief, over time and with the support of others you will come to experience what I like to describe as "reconciliation." When you come out on the other side of the wilderness and you are able to fully enjoy life and living again, you have achieved reconciliation of your grief. You will learn more about this important concept in Touchstone Nine. But before we get there, let's explore some of the other trail markers to watch for on your path to healing.

Recognize You
Are Not Crazy

*"If you are sure you understand
everything that is going on, you
are hopelessly confused."*

- Walter Mondale

In all my years as a grief counselor, the most common question mourners have asked me is, "Am I going crazy?" The second most common question is, "Am I normal?" The journey through grief can be so radically different from our everyday realities that sometimes it feels more like being picked up and dropped onto the surface of the moon than it does a trek through the wilderness.

Experiencing something that may seem "crazy" can be a very natural response when coping with the trauma of the death, and particularly with the uniquely devastating trauma of suicide.

This Touchstone helps you be on the lookout for the trail marker that affirms your sanity: Recognize You Are Not Crazy. It's an important trail marker, because if you miss it, your entire journey through the wilderness of your grief may feel like Alice's surreal visit to Wonderland.

Following are a number of common thoughts and feelings in grief that cause mourners to feel like they're going crazy. They may or may not be part of your personal experience.

Sudden Changes in Mood

The grief that comes with this journey can make you feel like you are surviving fairly well one minute and in the depths of despair the next. Your mood changes can be set off by driving past a familiar place, the lyrics of a song, an insensitive comment, a change in the weather, or simply waking up in the morning to a new day without this person in your life.

Be patient with yourself. As you do the work of mourning and receive the support you deserve, the periods of despair and darkness will be interspersed with more periods of lightness and hope.

Memory Lapses and Time Distortion

Long-term memory may still be with you, but short-term memory—such as what you did yesterday or where you just put something—often goes away. Time may also feel very distorted, meaning that sometimes, time moves quickly; at other times, it crawls. You may lose track of what day, month, or even year it is.

Polyphasic Behavior and Thinking Challenges

This is a fancy-sounding term that means you start doing something and then, right in the middle of it, you forget what you are doing and start doing something else. These kinds of scattered behaviors often go hand-in-hand with an inability to stay focused. Again, you will need to be self-compassionate and patient before you see these experiences soften ever so slowly over time.

Psychic Numbing, Dissociation, and Disconnection

Psychic numbing is like a bandage that your psyche has placed over your wound. The bandage protects the wound until it becomes less raw and open. This has been described to me as "watching myself from the outside in."

Dissociation is a close cousin of psychic numbing. It is where your emotions are split off from your thoughts because they are too overwhelming to encounter.

Disconnection is also common in suicide grief. When someone dies from natural causes such as old age, it is sometimes easier to retain happy memories than with a death from a suicide. Your connection to happy memories may be more complicated. Because the person seems to have made a choice that is so painful to you, you may be more at risk for being disconnected from happy memories. Let me assure you that you can and will be able to restore happy memories of your loved person, but in the meantime, go slow and reach out to compassionate people who will support you.

Self-focus or Feeling Selfish

Especially early in your grief, you may find yourself less conscious of the needs of others. You may not want to listen to other people's life problems, feeling they pale in comparison to your own. You may not have the energy to attend to the needs of your children or family. This doesn't mean you are crazy or selfish. What it does mean is that you have emotional and spiritual needs that are demanding your attention and energy right now.

Rethinking and Restorative Retelling of the Story

Whether you are conscious of it or not, you retell yourself and others the story in an effort to help yourself integrate the death into your life. What you have experienced—the death of someone you love to suicide—is so difficult to fathom that your mind compels you to revisit it again and again until you have truly acknowledged and embraced its presence. Allow yourself this necessary review. Don't be upset with yourself if you cannot seem to stop repeating your story, whether in your mind or aloud to others.

Powerlessness and Helplessness

The trauma of suicide grief can at times leave you feeling powerless. You may think or say, "What am I going to do? I feel so completely helpless." While part of you realizes you had no control over what happened, another part might feel a sense of powerlessness at not having been able to prevent it.

Your "if onlys" and "what ifs" are often expressions of wishing you could have been more powerful or in control of something you could not. Lack of control is a difficult reality to accept, yet it is one that, over time and through the work of mourning, you must encounter.

Loss of Energy and the Lethargy of Grief

Experiencing trauma grief is physically demanding. You may well lack energy and feel highly fatigued and weak. You are probably not sleeping very well, and your appetite may be affected, with either lack of desire to eat or the tendency to overeat. You may be more susceptible to illness and physical discomforts. Your body has special needs right now and will keep asking you to take good care of it.

A Feeling of Before the Suicide and After the Suicide

When someone precious to you takes his or her own life, there is a Before and an After. There is your life Before the suicide, and now there is your life After the suicide. It's as if your internal calendar gets reset to mark the significance of the profound loss.

Some, certainly not all, people I have counseled at my Center for Loss have told me, without much thought or conscious calculation, they know how many years, months, and days it has been since the suicide death. This new way of keeping time is perfectly natural. Your mind and heart have simply come up with a new system to mark the earth's relentless motion.

Expressing Feelings More Openly Than in the Past

This sudden, tragic death sometimes makes you more aware of how love makes the world go round. Now you may find yourself not sitting on feelings you do have and being more expressive to people you care deeply about.

You may now discover that three simple yet profound words—I love you—have deep, spiritual meaning to you. Where in the past you may have hesitated to say them, they may now come easily from your lips.

Griefbursts, Pangs, or Spasms

You may think that long periods of deep sadness make up the bulk of this journey into grief. Actually, you may more frequently encounter acute and episodic "pangs" or "spasms" of grief that come at you in a wave-like fashion.

During a griefburst, you may feel an overwhelming sense of missing aspects of what once was and find yourself openly crying, sometimes sobbing uncontrollably. These griefbursts may make you feel crazy, but rest assured, you are not! If, and more likely when, one strikes you, be compassionate with yourself. You have every right to miss your special person and feel temporary paralysis or loss of control.

Crying and Sobbing

If you're crying and sobbing a lot, you may feel like you never will stop, which can trigger your feelings of going crazy. But sobbing is an expression of the deep, strong emotions within you. These emotions need to get out, and sobbing allows for their release. Cry, wail, and sob as long and as hard and as often as you need to. Tears have a voice of their own. Let your tears speak, listen to the tears, and heal.

Borrowed Tears

Borrowed tears seem to come out of nowhere and are triggered by something you don't associate with the person you're mourning the loss of and wouldn't normally have been upset by. You're crying because your heart and soul are hurting and your emotions are tender. Think of it this way: If you press on your leg gently with your hand, it doesn't hurt. But if you break your leg and then press on it, even the slightest touch can hurt. You heart is broken now, and anything that touches it even slightly may hurt. This is normal and will pass as your heart continues to heal.

Linking Objects and Memorabilia

Linking objects are items that belonged to the dead person that you now like to have around you. If you like to hold, be near, look at, sleep with, caress, even smell a special belonging of the person who is dead, you're not crazy. You're simply trying to hold on to a tangible, physical connection to the person.

When the death is from suicide, I often find that you need to keep belongings close to you longer than many people around you may be comfortable with. But don't let them rush you out of their needs instead of yours. Go at your own pace and remember—once you have given something away or disposed of it, you often cannot get it back.

Carried Grief from Prior Losses

Some people, through no fault of their own, carry longstanding and cumulative grief, often stemming from their childhood. Now, as you experience this death and the need to mourn, you may have some symptoms (such as generalized anxiety, panic attacks, depression) that are invitations to go backward and give attention to prior losses that were never fully mourned and integrated into your life. Sometimes you cannot mourn current losses and life transitions until you go backward and work on carried grief.

Suicidal Thoughts

Thoughts that come and go about questioning if you want to go on living can be a normal part of your grief and mourning. Usually these thoughts are not so much an active wish to kill yourself as they are a wish to avoid or ease your pain.

To have these thoughts is normal and not crazy; however, to make plans and take action to end your life is extremely concerning and not a normal response to this tragic death. If thoughts of suicide take on planning and structure, make certain that you get help immediately. Also keep a close watch on other close friends and family members grieving this death.

Dreams or Nightmares

Dreams are one of the ways the work of mourning takes place. A dream may reflect a searching for the person who has died, for example. You may dream that you are with the person in a crowded place and lose him and cannot find him. Dreams also provide opportunities—to feel close to the person who died, to embrace the reality of the death, to gently confront the depth of the loss, to renew memories, or to develop a new self-identity. Dreams also may help you search for meaning in life and death or explore unfinished business. Finally, dreams can show you hope for the future.

It is one thing to dream, it is another to experience nightmares that frighten and disturb you. Nightmares can make you feel crazy, and if they are part of your experience, I urge you to see a professional caregiver who can help you sort out what is going on.

Mystical Experiences

The primary form of mystical experience that mourners who have experienced a suicide death have shared with me involves some sense of communication to or from the dead person. I have listened to and learned from hundreds of people who have seen, heard, and felt the presence of someone who has died. If you do have any of these mystical experiences, I hope they bring you comfort and hope.

Anniversary and Holiday Grief Occasions

Naturally, anniversary and holiday occasions can bring about pangs of grief. Birthdays, wedding dates, holidays such as Easter, Thanksgiving, Hanukkah, and Christmas, and other special occasions create a heightened sense of loss. At these times, you may likely experience griefbursts.

If you're having a really tough time on special days, you're not crazy. Perhaps the most important thing to remember is that your feelings are natural. And sometimes the anticipation of an anniversary or holiday turns out to be worse than the day itself.

Ritual-Stimulated Reactions, Seasonal Reactions, Music-Stimulated Reactions, and Age-Correspondence Reactions

Similar to griefbursts in nature, certain experiences you encounter might re-stimulate feelings surrounding your loss.

- Ritual-stimulated reactions stem from things like gathering for family dinners or a Sunday brunch. You may have been used to this being a special time with your precious person and naturally feel his or her absence.

- Seasonal reactions relate to how the change of seasons can stimulate grief. Be gentle with yourself if you know you are more prone to being depressed at a particular time of year.

- Music-stimulated grief relates to how music can activate your right brain, creating associations and deep, often profound feelings stimulated by a specific song or piece of music.

- Age-correspondence reactions can take place, for example, when you reach the age of the person who took his or her own life. So, if your parent died at age 62, when you reach that age you may naturally experience a renewed sense of loss.

You're Not Crazy, You're Grieving and Mourning

Never forget that your journey through the wilderness of your grief may bring you through all kinds of strange and unfamiliar terrain. When it seems like you're going crazy, remind yourself to look for the trail marker that assures you you're not going crazy, you're grieving and mourning.

Understand the Six
Needs of Mourning

"Mourning is a series of spiritual awakenings borne out of the willingness to experience an authentic encounter with the pain surrounding the loss."

– Alan D. Wolfelt

If you are looking for a detailed map for your journey through suicide grief, none exists. *Your* wilderness is an undiscovered wilderness and you its first explorer.

However, when we are mourning a death to suicide, we do have some similar needs. Instead of referring to stages of grief, I say that we as mourners have six central needs. In the Introduction I said that as we journey through grief, we need to follow the trail markers, or the Touchstones, if we are to find our way out of the wilderness. The trail marker we will discuss in this chapter explores the six central needs of mourning. You might think of Touchstone Six as its own little grouping of trail markers.

Mourning Need 1: Accept the Reality of the Death

You can know something in your head but not in your heart. This is what often happens when someone you love takes his or her own life. This first need of mourning, a close cousin to Touchstone One (open to the presence of your loss), involves gently confronting the reality that someone you care about will never physically return to your life again.

Because the nature of a suicide death is sudden and naturally traumatic, acknowledging the full reality usually doesn't happen in days, but in weeks or even months. To survive you will probably naturally need to push away the reality of the death at times.

One moment the reality of the loss may be tolerable; another moment it may be unbearable. Be patient with this need. Remember—this first need of mourning, like the other five that follow, may intermittently require your attention for months. Be compassionate with yourself as you work on each of them.

Mourning Need 2: Let Yourself Feel the Pain of the Loss

You will probably discover that you need to dose yourself in embracing your pain. In other words, you cannot (nor should you try to) overload yourself with the hurt all at one time. Sometimes you may need to distract yourself from the pain of the death, while at other times you will need to create a safe place to move toward it.

Unfortunately, as I have said, our culture tends to encourage the denial of pain. We misunderstand the role of suffering. If you openly express your feelings of grief, misinformed friends may advise you to "carry on" or "keep your chin up." If, on the other hand, you remain "strong" and "in control," you may be congratulated for "doing well" with your grief. Actually, doing well with your grief means becoming well acquainted with your pain.

Never forget that suicide grief is usually a slow, arduous experience. Your pain will probably ebb and flow for months, even years; embracing it when it washes over you will require patience, support, and strength.

Mourning Need 3: Remember the Person Who Died

Do you have any kind of relationship with people after they die? Of course. You have a relationship of memory. Precious memories, dreams reflecting the significance of the relationship, and objects that link you to the person who died (such as photos, souvenirs, clothing, etc.) are examples of some of the things that give testimony to a different form of a continued relationship.

Embracing your memories can be a very slow and, at times, painful process that occurs in small steps. Remember—

don't try to do all your work of mourning at once. Go slowly and be patient with yourself.

Following are a few examples of things you can do to keep memories alive while embracing the reality that the person has died:

- Talking out or writing out favorite memories
- Giving yourself permission to keep some special keepsakes or "linking objects"
- Displaying photos of the person who is now dead
- Visiting places of special significance that stimulate memories of times shared together
- Reviewing photo albums at special times such as holidays, birthdays, and anniversaries

In my experience, remembering the past makes hoping for the future possible. Your future will become open to new experiences only to the extent that you embrace the past.

Mourning Need 4: Develop a New Self-Identity

Your personal identity, or self-perception, is the result of the ongoing process of establishing a sense of who you are.

Part of your self-identity comes from the relationships you have with other people. When someone with whom you have a relationship dies, your self-identity, or the way you see yourself, naturally changes.

You may have gone from being a "wife" or "husband" to a "widow" or "widower." You may have gone from being a "parent" to a "bereaved parent." The way you define yourself and the way society defines you is changed.

You may occasionally feel child-like as you struggle with your changing identity. You may feel a temporarily heightened dependence on others as well as feelings of helplessness, frustration, inadequacy, and fear. These feelings can be overwhelming and scary, but they are actually a natural response to this important need of mourning.

Remember—do what you need to do in order to survive, at least for now, as you try to re-anchor yourself. To be dependent on others as you struggle with a changed identity does not make you weak, bad, or inferior. Your self-identity has been assaulted. Be compassionate with yourself. Accept the support of others.

Many people discover that as they work on this need, they ultimately discover some positive aspects of their changed self-identity. You may develop a renewed confidence in yourself. You may develop an assertive part of your identity that empowers you to go on living even though you continue to feel a sense of loss.

Mourning Need 5: Search for Meaning

When someone you love takes his or her own life, you naturally question the meaning and purpose of life. "How could God let this happen?" "Why did this happen now, in this way?"

As Edward K. Rynearson wisely noted following his wife Julie's death to suicide, "While religious or spiritual concepts might have prepared me for Julie's death, they could not prepare me for her violent dying. There is no spiritual belief or religion, despite any scripture or hymn or sermon, that finds order or meaning in a violent death."

At times, overwhelming sadness and loneliness may be your constant companions. You may feel that when this person died, part of you died with him or her. And now you are faced with finding some meaning in going on with your life even though you may often feel so empty.

You might feel distant from your God or Higher Power, even questioning the very existence of God. Such feelings of doubt are normal.

Move at your own pace as you recognize that allowing yourself to hurt and find continued reason to live are not mutually exclusive. More often, your need to mourn and your need to find meaning in your continued living will blend into each other, with the former very slowly giving way to the latter as healing occurs.

Mourning Need 6: Let Others Help You—Now and Always

The quality and quantity of understanding support you get during your work of mourning will have a major influence on your capacity to heal. You cannot—nor should you try to—do this alone. Drawing on the experiences and encouragement of friends, fellow mourners, or professional counselors is not a weakness but a healthy human need. And because mourning is a process that takes place over time, this support must be available months and even years after the suicide death of someone in your life.

Unfortunately, many bereaved people are abandoned shortly after the event of the death. "It's best not to talk about death," "It's over and done with," and "It's time to get on with your life" are the types of messages directed at grieving people, particularly when suicide is the cause of the death. Obviously, these messages encourage you to deny or repress your grief rather than express it.

To be truly helpful, the people in your support system must appreciate the impact this death has had on you. They must understand that in order to heal, you must be allowed—even encouraged—to mourn long after the death. And they must encourage you to see mourning not as an enemy to be vanquished, but as a necessity to be experienced as a result of having loved.

Nurture Yourself

"Getting better means being patient with oneself when progress is slow... It means finding safe, supportive persons with whom to share the pain."

– Janice Harris Lord

This Touchstone is a reminder to be kind to yourself as you journey through the wilderness of your grief. Be gentle with yourself. You are naturally fragile and vulnerable. You can give attention to your wounds by making decisions that ultimately contribute to your healing. Be assured that there will come a time when your grief will not be overwhelming and when you really do live once more. In the meantime, please allow me the honor of trying to help you with your self-care needs.

If you were embarking on a hike of many days through the mountains of Colorado, would you dress scantily, carry little water, and push yourself until you dropped? Of course not. You would prepare carefully and proceed cautiously. You would take care of yourself because if you didn't, you could die. The consequence of not taking care of yourself as you grieve and mourn this death can be equally devastating.

Over many years of walking with hundreds of people in the wilderness of suicide grief, I have discovered that many of us are hard on ourselves during this time in our lives. Yet good self-care is essential to your survival. Practicing good self-care doesn't mean you are feeling sorry for yourself, being selfish, or being self-indulgent; rather, it means you are creating conditions that allow you to integrate the transformation that this suicide brings into your heart and soul.

The grief that comes with a suicide death invites you to embrace each precious moment of life and to care deeply for your family and friends. Suicide grief invites you to find hidden treasures everywhere—a child's toothless smile, a beautiful sunrise, the smell of fresh flowers, a friend's gentle touch. In caring for yourself and tending to your special needs right this moment, you will go on to discover the capacity to live your life with purpose and meaning every moment of every day.

Nurturing Yourself in Five Important Realms

When we are "torn apart" by suicide grief, one of our most important special needs is to nurture ourselves in five important areas: physically; emotionally, cognitively; socially; and spiritually.

The Physical Realm

Your body may be letting you know it feels distressed. Actually, one literal definition of the word "grievous" is "causing physical suffering." You may be shocked by how much your body responds to the impact of your loss.

Among the most common physical responses to loss are troubles with sleeping and low energy. You may have difficulty getting to sleep. Perhaps even more commonly, you may wake up early in the morning and have trouble getting back to sleep. During your grief journey, your body needs more rest than usual. You may also find yourself getting tired more quickly, sometimes even at the start of the day.

Muscle aches and pains, shortness of breath, feelings of emptiness in your stomach, tightness in your throat or chest, digestive problems, sensitivity to noise, heart palpitations, queasiness, nausea, headaches, increased allergic reactions, changes in appetite, weight loss or gain, agitation, and generalized tension—these are all ways your body may react to the death of someone loved.

If you have a chronic existing health problem, it may become worse. The stress of grief can suppress your immune system and make you more susceptible to physical problems.

Good self-care is important at this time. The quality of your life ahead depends on how you take care of your body today. The lethargy of grief you are probably experiencing is a natural mechanism intended to slow you down and encourage you to care for your body.

And be certain to talk out your grief. Many grieving people have taught me that if they avoid or repress talking about the death, their bodies will begin to express their grief for them.

The Emotional Realm

We explored in Touchstone Four a multitude of emotions that are often part of grief and mourning. These emotions reflect that you have special needs that require support from both outside yourself and inside yourself. Becoming familiar with the terrain of these emotions can and will help you authentically mourn and heal in small doses over time. The important thing to remember is that we honor our emotions when we give attention to them.

The Cognitive Realm

Your mind is the intellectual ability to think, absorb information, make decisions, and reason logically. Without doubt, you have special needs in the cognitive realm of your grief experience. Just as your body and emotions let you know you have experienced being torn apart, your mind has also, in effect, been torn apart.

Thinking normally after the suicide death of someone precious to you would be very unlikely. Don't be surprised if you struggle with short-term memory problems, have trouble making even simple decisions, and think you may be going crazy. Essentially, your mind is in a state of disorientation and confusion.

The Social Realm

The suicide death of someone you love has resulted in a very real disconnection from the world around you. When you reach out and connect with your family and friends, you are beginning to reconnect. By being aware of the larger picture, one that includes all the people in your life, you gain some perspective. You recognize you are part of a greater whole, and that recognition can empower you. You open up your heart to love again when you reach out to others. Your link to family, friends, and community is vital for your sense of well-being and belonging.

If you don't nurture the warm, loving relationships that still exist in your life, you will probably continue to feel disconnected and isolated. You may even withdraw into your own small world and grieve but not mourn. Isolation can then become the barrier that keeps your grief from softening over time. You will begin to die while you are still alive. Allow your friends and family to nurture you. Let them in and rejoice in the connection.

The Spiritual Realm

Let me assure you that I realize the word *spiritual* has many different meanings to different people. The survivors of suicide I have companioned have taught me that each person's spiritual journey is unique and sustained by your individual beliefs and values. The suicide death of someone precious to you becomes part of the *mystery* and is not something you can quickly and easily understand. You might find it helpful to remember that *mystery* was the ancient name for God.

For our purpose here, I think of spirituality as the collection of beliefs about our existence. Obviously, when someone takes his or her own life, you are invited into some spiritual questions for which there are no easy answers: "Why did this happen?" "Will my life be worth living again?" You may feel a loss of faith or doubt or feel distant from any sense of spirituality. Yes, sometimes the irony of believing involves doubting, and suicide can naturally engage you in doubting. That is why, if I could, I would encourage all of us when we are in the midst of the grief that accompanies suicide to put down "Nurture my spirit" first on our daily to-do lists.

You probably recognize, as I do, that spirituality and religiosity are not synonymous. In some people's lives they overlap completely; their religious lives *are* their spiritual lives. Other people have a rich spiritual life with few or no ties to organized religion. Obviously, each of us defines our own spirituality in the depths of our own hearts and minds. The paths we choose will be our own, discovered through self-examination, reflection, and spiritual transformation.

I do personally believe that even in your grief, you can still befriend *hope* (if I didn't believe this I could not function in my helping role at my Center for Loss or support survivors of suicide deaths), and that even the most ordinary moment can feed your soul. In some ways, spirituality is anchored in faith, which is expecting some goodness even in the worst of times. It is not about fear, which is expecting the worst even in the best of times. Spirituality reminds you that you can and will integrate losses into your life, that there is goodness in others, and that there are many pathways to Heaven.

If you have doubts about your capacity to connect with your spirituality, your religion, or your God right now, try to approach the world with the openness of a child. Embrace the support you can experience from the simple things in life: the unexpected kindness of a stranger; a sunrise or sunset; the rustle of the wind in the trees. Even in the face of your devastating loss, you can and will find yourself discovering the essentials within your soul and spirit of the world around you.

Reach Out for Help

"At times our light goes out and is rekindled by a spark from another person."

– *Albert Schweitzer*

Surviving the death of someone precious in your life catapults you into a wilderness experience filled with shock, disorientation and confusion, and chaos. I recognize that reaching out for help is more challenging than many people think. Early on in your journey, you may be doing well to just breathe in and breathe out, let alone make a thoughtful decision to get help from friends, family, support groups, or professional caregivers.

Yet perhaps the most compassionate thing you can do for yourself at this vulnerable, overwhelming time is to reach out to others for help. Think of it this way: Grieving and mourning the death of someone precious to suicide is probably the hardest work you have ever done. And hard work is less burdensome when others lend a hand.

Seek out the support of the people in your life who are naturally good helpers. A few shoulders to cry on and some listening ears can make all the difference in the world. Reaching out for help also connects you to other people and strengthens the bonds of love that make life worth living again.

Also, when you do ask for help, you have to open your heart and soul to be available to receive the help. You have to ask for the help, believe you are deserving of the help, and then receive the help.

Where to Turn for Help

Fellow Survivors: You may well find some of your most compassionate support comes from other suicide survivors. In their company, you can express your grief openly without fear of judgment. You will often discover you speak the same language and can instinctively retell your story as much as you need to.

Select Friends and Family: The caring, warmth, and support of the "right" friends and family can go a long way in helping you. Sometimes, even a few compassionate friends and family who are gifted with effective listening ears can make all the difference in the world.

Support Groups: In these groups, each person shares his or her unique grief journey in a non-threatening, safe atmosphere. Over time, many participants report feeling like "family." Group members are usually very patient with you and your grief and encourage the sacred retelling of your story.

Your Religious or Spiritual Community: The grief from suicide may set you off on a spiritual pilgrimage. Search out and locate compassionate sources of support and understanding. Avoid any persons of faith who purport that suicide leads to damnation. Unfortunately, there are still a few of those people out there. Fortunately, there are some excellent spiritual places and people who can and will help you get the support you deserve.

A Professional Counselor or Caregiver: A professional counselor may be a very helpful addition to your support system. There is no shame or weakness in seeing a counselor. On the contrary, it takes wisdom to realize you would benefit from this kind of help.

You will know you may have found the right counselor when you feel safe, can be open and honest, and your spirit feels "at home."

Dr. Wolfelt's Rule of Thirds

In my own grief experiences and in the lives of people I have been privileged to counsel, I have discovered that in general, you can take all the people in your life and divide them into thirds when it comes to grief support.

One third of the people in your life will turn out to be neutral in response to your grief experience. They will neither help nor hinder you in your journey.

Another third of the people in your life will turn out to be harmful to you in your efforts to integrate the grief and loss into your life. While they are usually not setting out to intentionally harm you, they will judge you, minimize your experience, or pull you off your path to eventual healing.

And the final third of people in your life will turn out to be truly supportive helpers. They will demonstrate a desire to understand you and the experience you are going through. They will be willing to be involved in your pain and suffering without feeling the need to take it away from you. They will believe in your capacity to integrate this grief into your life and eventually go on to live a life of meaning and purpose.

Seek out your friends, family, and caregivers who fall into the last third. They will be your confidants and momentum-givers on your journey. When you are in the wilderness of suicide grief, try to avoid that second third, for they will trip you up and cause you to fall. They may even light up a wildfire right there in the midst of your wilderness!

Safe People: Three Fundamental Helping Roles

While there are a multitude of ways that people who care about you might reach out to help you, here are three important and fundamental helping roles. Effective helpers will help you:

1. *Feel companioned during your journey.* Those who companion you are willing and able to affirm your pain and suffering. They are able to sit with you and the feelings that surface as you walk through the wilderness.

2. *Encounter your feelings related to the suicide death.* These are people who understand the need for you to tell

your account of your grief experience. They gently invite you to tell your story and provide a safe place for you to openly express your many thoughts and feelings.

3. *Embrace hope.* These are people who help you sustain the presence of hope—an expectation of a good that is yet to be. They do not force the concept of hope upon you but rather gently embody joy and hopefulness. They can be present to you and affirm your goodness, while all the time helping you trust in yourself that you can and will heal.

A Final Word About Reaching Out for Help

As a grief counselor, I have been honored to companion hundreds of people who have been touched and changed when someone precious to them has taken his or her own life. Among the important lessons they have taught me is that sharing their grief with others is an integral part of the eventual healing process.

Seek Reconciliation, Not Resolution

*"Unless you believe you are worthy
of reconciliation and healing your
suicide grief, you will question it,
inhibit it, deny it, or push it away."*

– Alan D. Wolfelt

How do you ever find your way out of the wilderness of your grief? You don't have to dwell there forever, do you?

The good news is that no, you don't have to dwell there forever. If you follow the trail markers on your journey through the wilderness, you will find your way out. But just as with any significant experience in your life, the wilderness will always live inside you and be a part of who you are.

A number of psychological models describing grief refer to "resolution," "recovery," "reestablishment," or "reorganization" as being the destination of your grief journey. You may have heard—indeed you may believe—that your grief journey's end will come when you resolve, or recover from, your grief.

But you may also be coming to understand one of the fundamental truths of grief: Your journey will never truly end. People do not "get over" grief. My personal and professional experience tells me that a total return to "normalcy" after the death of someone loved is not possible; we are all forever changed by the experience of grief.

Reconciliation is a term I find more appropriate for what occurs as you work to integrate the new reality of moving forward in life without the physical presence of the person who died. With reconciliation comes a renewed sense of energy and confidence, an ability to fully acknowledge the reality of the death, and a capacity to become re-involved in the activities of living. There is also an acknowledgment that pain and grief are difficult, yet necessary, parts of life.

As the experience of reconciliation unfolds, you will recognize that life is and will continue to be different without the presence of the person who died. Changing the relationship with the person who died from one of presence to one of memory and redirecting one's energy and initiative toward the future often take longer—and involve more hard work—than most people are aware. We, as human beings, never resolve our grief, but instead become reconciled to it.

We come to reconciliation in our grief journey when the full reality of the death becomes a part of us. Beyond an intellectual working through of the death, there is also an emotional and spiritual working through. What had been understood at the head level is now understood at the heart level.

Signs of Reconciliation

How do you know if you are moving toward reconciling your loss? Here are some signs to look for that let you know that you are making progress in your journey through the wilderness of suicide grief.

- A recognition of the reality and finality of the death.
- A return to stable eating and sleeping patterns.
- A renewed sense of release from the person who has died. You will have thoughts about the person, but you will not be preoccupied by these thoughts.
- The capacity to enjoy experiences in life that are normally enjoyable.
- The establishment of new and healthy relationships.
- The capacity to live a full life without feelings of guilt or lack of self-respect.
- The drive to organize and plan one's life toward the future.

- The serenity to become comfortable with the way things are rather than attempting to make things as they were.
- The versatility to welcome more change in your life.
- The awareness that you have allowed yourself to fully mourn and you have survived.
- The awareness that you do not "get over" your grief; instead, you have a new reality, meaning, and purpose in your life.
- The acquaintance of new parts of yourself that you have discovered in your grief journey.
- The adjustment to new role changes that have resulted from the loss of the relationship.
- The acknowledgment that the pain of loss is an inherent part of life resulting from the ability to give and receive love.

Reconciliation emerges much in the way grass grows. Usually we don't check our lawns daily to see if the grass is growing, but it does grow, and soon we come to realize it's time to mow the grass again. Likewise, we don't look at ourselves each day as mourners to see how we are healing.

Yet we do come to realize, over the course of months and years, that we have come a long way.

Usually there is not one great moment of arrival, but rather subtle changes and small advancements. It's helpful to have gratitude for even very small steps forward. If you are beginning to taste your food again, be thankful. If you mustered the energy to meet your friend for lunch, be grateful. If you finally got a good night's sleep, rejoice.

One of my greatest teachers, C.S. Lewis, wrote in *A Grief Observed* about his grief symptoms as they eased in his journey to reconciliation:

There was no sudden, striking, and emotional transition. Like the warming of a room or the coming of daylight, when you first notice them they have already been going on for some time.

Of course, you will take some steps backward from time to time, but that is to be expected. Keep believing in yourself. Set your intention to reconcile your grief and have hope that you can and will come to live and love again.

Appreciate Your Transformation

"Nature does not know extinction,
all it knows is transformation."

– Wernher Von Braun

The journey through the grief that follows the death of someone precious to suicide is life-changing. I'm certain you have discovered that you have been transformed by your journey into grief. Transformation literally means an entire change in form. Many mourners have said to me, "I have grown from this experience. I am a different person."

Now, don't take me the wrong way. Believe me, I understand that the growth resulted from something you would have preferred to avoid. While I have come to believe that our greatest gifts often come from our wounds, these are not wounds we masochistically go looking for. When others offer untimely comments like, "You'll grow from this," your right to be hurt, angry, or deeply sad is taken away from you.

Growth Means Change

We as human beings are forever changed by the suicide death of someone in our lives. You may discover that you have developed new attitudes. You may be more patient or more sensitive to the feelings and circumstances of others, especially those suffering from loss. You may have new insights that guide the way you live your new life. You may have developed new skills or ways of viewing humankind or the world around you.

Growth Means a New Inner Balance with No End Points

While you may do your work of mourning in ways that help you recapture some sense of inner balance, it is a *new* inner balance. The word growth reflects that you do not reach some final end point in your grief journey.

Growth Means Exploring Your Assumptions About Life

The death of someone to suicide invites you to look at your assumptions about life. Your loss experiences have a tendency to transform your assumptions, values, and priorities. Every loss in life calls out for a new search for meaning, including a natural struggle with spiritual concerns, often transforming your vision of your God and your faith life.

Growth Means Utilizing Your Potential

In some ways, death loss seems to free the potential within. Questions such as "Who am I? What am I meant to do with my life?" often naturally arise during grief. Answering them inspires a hunt. You may find yourself searching for your very soul.

Your Responsibility to Live

Sorrow is an inseparable dimension of our human experience. We suffer after a loss because we are human. And in our suffering, we are transformed. While it hurts to suffer lost love, the alternative is apathy, which literally means the inability to suffer, and it results in a lifestyle that avoids human relationship to avoid suffering.

Perhaps you have noticed that some people die a long time before they stop breathing. They have no more promises to keep, no more people to love, no more places to go. It is as if the souls of these people have already died. Don't let this happen to you. You have to live not only for yourself, but for the precious person in your life who has died—to work on his or her unfinished work and to realize his or her unfinished dreams.

What if the person who died could return to see what you are doing with your life? *No matter how deep your grief or how anguished your soul, bereavement does not free you from your responsibility to live until you die. The gift of life is so precious and fragile. Choose life!*

Carrying Your Transformation Forward

Tomorrow is now. It is here. It is waiting for you. You have many choices in living the transformation that grief has brought to your life.

You can choose to visualize your heart opening each and every day. When your heart is open, you are receptive to what life brings you, both happy and sad. By "staying open," you create a gateway to your healing.

When this happens you will know that the long nights of suffering in the wilderness have given way to a journey towards the dawn. You will know that new life has come as you celebrate the first rays of a new light and new beginning. Choose life!

As you continue to experience how grief has transformed you, be open to the new directions your life is now taking. You have learned to watch for trail markers in your continued living. Listen to the wisdom of your inner voice. Make choices that are congruent with what you have learned on your journey. Say "YES" to life and "NO" to suicide. Bless you. I hope we meet one day.

The Suicide Survivor's Bill of Rights

Someone you love has ended his or her own life. Your grief is unique and profound, and you have special needs that must be tended to in the coming weeks, months, and years. Though you should reach out to others as you do the work of mourning, you should not feel obligated to accept the unhelpful responses you may receive from some people. You are the one who is grieving, and as such, you have certain "rights" no one should try to take away from you.

The following list is intended both to empower you to heal and to decide how others can and cannot help. This is not to discourage you from reaching out to others for help, but rather to assist you in distinguishing useful responses from hurtful ones.

1. **I have the right to experience my own unique grief.**
   No one else will grieve this death in exactly the same way I do. So, when I turn to others for help, I will not allow them to tell me what I should or should not be thinking, feeling, or doing.

2. **I have the right to talk about my grief.** Talking about my grief and the story of the death will help me heal. I will seek out others who will allow me to talk as much as I want, as often as I want, and who will listen without judging. If at times I don't feel like talking, I also have the right to be silent, although I understand that bottling everything up inside will prevent my healing.

3. **I have the right to feel a multitude of emotions.** Confusion, disorientation, fear, shame, anger, and guilt are just a few of the emotions I might feel as part of my grief journey. Others may try to tell me that what I do feel is wrong, but I know that my feelings aren't right or wrong, they just are.

4. **I have the right to work through any feelings of guilt and relinquish responsibility.** I may feel guilty about this death, even though it was in no way my fault. I must come to acknowledge that the only person truly responsible was the person who took his or her own life. Still, I must feel and explore any possible feelings of guilt I may have in order to move beyond them.

5. **I have the right to know what can be known about what happened.** I can cope with what I know or understand, but it is much harder to cope with the unknown. If I have questions about the death, I have the right to have those questions answered honestly and thoroughly by those who may have the information I seek.

6. **I have the right to embrace the mystery.** It is normal and natural for me to want to understand why the person I love took his or her own life, but I also have the right to accept that I may never fully and truly understand. I will naturally search for meaning, but I will also "stand under" the unknowable mystery of life and death.

7. **I have the right to embrace my spirituality.** I will embrace and express my spirituality in ways that feel right to me. I will spend time in the company of people who understand and support my spiritual or religious beliefs. If I feel angry at God or find myself questioning my faith or beliefs, that's OK. I will find someone to talk with who won't be critical of my feelings of hurt and abandonment.

8. **I have the right to treasure my memories.** Memories are one of the best legacies that exist after the death of someone loved. I will always remember. If at first my memories are dominated by thoughts of the death itself, I will realize that this is a normal and necessary step on the path to healing. Over time, I know I will be able to remember the love and the good times.

9. **I have the right to hope.** Hope is an expectation of a good that is yet to be. I have the need and the right to have hope for my continued life. I can have hope and joy in my life and still miss and love the person who died.

10. **I have the right to move toward my grief and heal.** Reconciling my grief will not happen quickly. Grief is a process, not an event. I will be patient and tolerant with myself and avoid people who are impatient and intolerant with me. I must help those around me understand that the suicide death of someone loved has changed my life forever.

About the Author

Author, educator, and grief counselor
Dr. Alan Wolfelt is known across
North America for his compassionate
philosophy of "companioning" versus
"treating" mourners. He is committed
to helping people mourn well so they
can go on to live well and love well.

Dr. Wolfelt is founder and Director of the Center
for Loss and Life Transition, located in the beautiful
mountain foothills of Fort Collins, Colorado. Past
recipient of the Association of Death Education and
Counseling's Death Educator Award, he is also a
faculty member of the University of Colorado Medical
School's Department of Family Medicine.

To contact Dr. Wolfelt about presenting in your
community or attending one of his educational retreats
for bereavement caregivers, please e-mail DrWolfelt@
centerforloss.com or call (970) 226-6050.